D

Pebble® Bilingüe/Bilingual Plus

Mira dentro/Look Inside

una cabaña

Log Cabin

por/by Mari Schuh

Editora consultora/Consulting Editor: Gail Saunders-Smith, PhD

Consultor/Consultant: John Mark Lambertson
Director y Archivista/Director and Archivist
National Frontier Trails Museum
Independence, Missouri

CAPSTONE PRESS
a capstone imprint

Pebble Plus is published by Capstone Press,
151 Good Counsel Drive, P.O. Box 669, Mankato, Minnesota 56002.
www.capstonepub.com

Books published by Capstone Press are manufactured with paper
containing at least 10 percent post-consumer waste.

Library of Congress Cataloging-in-Publication Data
Schuh, Mari C., 1975–
  [Look inside a log cabin. Spanish & English]
  Mira dentro de una cabaña / por Mari Schuh = Look inside a log cabin / by Mari Schuh.
    p. cm.—(Pebble plus bilingüe. Miro dentro = Pebble plus bilingual. Look inside)
  Text in Spanish and English.
  Includes index.
  Summary: "Simple text and photographs present American pioneer log cabins, their construction, and their
interaction with the environment—in both English and Spanish"—Provided by publisher.
  ISBN 978-1-4296-6909-2 (library binding)
  1. Log cabins—United States—History—Juvenile literature. 2. Pioneers—Dwellings—United States—History—
Juvenile literature. 3. Log cabins—United States—Design and construction—History—Juvenile literature.
4. Frontier and pioneer life—United States—Juvenile literature. I. Title. II. Title: Look inside a log cabin.
E179.5.S3418 2012
728.7'3—dc22   2011000649

Editorial Credits
Megan Peterson, editor; Strictly Spanish, translation services; Renée T. Doyle, designer; Danielle Ceminsky,
    bilingual book designer; Wanda Winch, media researcher; Laura Manthe, production specialist

Photo Credits
Alamy/Brad Mitchell, 13; Winston Fraser, 9
Capstone Press/Karon Dubke, 17, 21; Renée Doyle, back cover, 3
Gene K. Garrison Photography, 11
The Image Works/Jenny Hager, 15
North Wind Picture Archives, 7, 19
Shutterstock/Dmitry Kultayev, 24; Larisa Lofitskaya, 1, 22–23; Mary Terriberry, front cover
SuperStock, Inc./Richard Cummins, 5

Note to Parents and Teachers

The Mira dentro/Look Inside set supports national social studies standards related to
people, places, and culture. This book describes and illustrates log cabins in both English
and Spanish. The images support early readers in understanding the text. The repetition of
words and phrases helps early readers learn new words. This book also introduces early
readers to subject-specific vocabulary words, which are defined in the Glossary section.
Early readers may need assistance to read some words and to use the Table of Contents,
Glossary, Internet Sites, and Index sections of the book.

Printed in the United States of America in North Mankato, Minnesota.
032011
006110CGF11

Table of Contents

Tabla de Contenidos

What Is a Log Cabin?

A log cabin is a small home made of tree trunks. American pioneers built them as they moved west starting in the mid-1700s.

¿Qué es una cabaña?

Una cabaña es una casa pequeña hecha de troncos de árboles. Los pioneros americanos las construían mientras viajaban hacia el oeste a mediados de los años 1700.

Swedish pioneers built the
first log cabins in America.
They showed other pioneers
how to build them.

Pioneros suecos construyeron
las primeras cabañas de
troncos en América.
Ellos mostraron a otros
pioneros cómo construirlas.

Building a Log Cabin

To build a log cabin, pioneers

chopped down trees with an ax.

Then they cut notches in the

ends of the logs.

Cómo construir una cabaña

Para construir una cabaña, los

pioneros cortaban árboles con un

hacha. Luego, ellos cortaban muescas

en los extremos de los troncos.

Pioneers piled the logs to make walls. Then they used a process called chinking. They filled the wall spaces with mud, stones, and wood.

Los pioneros apilaban los troncos para hacer las paredes. Ellos usaban un proceso llamado rellenar. Ellos llenaban los espacios en las paredes con barro, piedras y madera.

Pioneers built a roof
with flat pieces of wood.

_____

Los pioneros construían
el techo con piezas
planas de madera.

Inside a Log Cabin

Most log cabins had only one room. Early cabins had windows covered with oiled paper. Later, windows were made of glass.

Dentro de una cabaña

La mayoría de las cabañas tiene sólo un cuarto. Las cabañas más antiguas tenían ventanas cubiertas con papel aceitado. Más adelante, las ventanas eran de vidrio.

The floors were made of dirt or wood. Pioneers slept near the roof in a loft.

Los pisos eran de tierra o de madera. Los pioneros dormían cerca del techo en un desván.

A stone fireplace kept the log cabin warm. Pioneers cooked food in the fireplace.

Una chimenea de piedra mantenía la cabaña caliente. Los pioneros cocinaban en la chimenea.

Log Cabins Today

You can learn about log cabins at parks and museums. See how pioneers lived in these strong wood homes.

Las cabañas hoy

Tú puedes aprender acerca de las cabañas en parques y museos. Fíjate cómo los pioneros vivían en estas fuertes casas de madera.

Glossary

ax—a tool with a sharp blade on the end of a handle, used to chop wood

chinking—the process of filling spaces between rows of logs with mud, stones, and small pieces of wood

loft—a space with a floor under the roof of a building

notch—a cut shaped like the letter "U" or "V"; pioneers cut notches into the ends of logs so the logs would join together

pioneer—a person who is among the first to settle in a new land

Swedish—people born in Sweden; Sweden is a country in northern Europe

Internet Sites

FactHound offers a safe, fun way to find Internet sites related to this book. All of the sites on FactHound have been researched by our staff.

Here's all you do:

Visit *www.facthound.com*

Type in this code: 9781429669092

Super-cool stuff!

Check out projects, games and lots more at
www.capstonekids.com

Glosario

el desván —un espacio con un piso bajo el techo de un edificio

la hacha—una herramienta con una cuchilla filosa en un extremo de un mango, usada para cortar madera

las muescas—un corte en forma de letra "U" o "V"; los pioneros cortaban muescas en los extremos de los troncos para poder unirlos

el pionero—una persona entre las primeras en habitar en una nueva tierra

rellenar—el proceso de llenar espacios entre hileras de troncos con barro, piedras y pedazos pequeños de madera

los suecos—las personas nacidas en Suecia; Suecia es un país en el norte de Europa

Sitios de Internet

FactHound brinda una forma segura y divertida de encontrar sitios de Internet relacionados con este libro. Todos los sitios en FactHound han sido investigados por nuestro personal.

Esto es todo lo que tienes que hacer:

Visita *www.facthound.com*

Ingresa este código: 9781429669092

¡Algo súper divertido! Hay proyectos, juegos y mucho más en **www.capstonekids.com**

Index

Índice